安徽师范大学

传媒视界丛书

陆青霖◎著

U0148380

瓷片上的中国

——影像·传播·价值

安徽师范大学出版社

ANHUI NORMAL UNIVERSITY PRESS

· 芜湖 ·

图书在版编目(CIP)数据

瓷片上的中国:影像·传播·价值 / 陆青霖著. —芜湖:安徽师范大学出版社,2021.1
(安徽师范大学传媒视界丛书)
ISBN 978-7-5676-4401-4

Ⅰ.①瓷… Ⅱ.①陆… Ⅲ.①青花瓷(考古) – 中国画 – 研究 – 景德镇 – 明清时代 Ⅳ.①K876.34②J212

中国版本图书馆CIP数据核字(2020)第204420号

本书由首批部校共建新闻学院专项经费资助出版

瓷片上的中国：影像·传播·价值

陆青霖◎著

责任编辑:胡志恒　王　贤
责任校对:吴　琼
装帧设计:丁奕奕
责任校对:桑国磊
出版发行:安徽师范大学出版社
　　　　芜湖市北京东路1号安徽师范大学赭山校区　　邮政编码:241000
网　　　址:http://www.ahnupress.com/
发 行 部:0553-3883578 5910327 5910310(传真)　E-mail:asdcbsfxb@126.com
印　　刷:安徽芜湖新华印务有限责任公司
版　　次:2021年1月第1版
印　　次:2021年1月第1次印刷
规　　格:880 mm×1230 mm　1/16
印　　张:6.75
字　　数:87千字
书　　号:ISBN 978-7-5676-4401-4
定　　价:109.00元

总　序

　　安徽师范大学新闻与传播学院成立于2010年5月，原名传媒学院，2015年1月改为现名。学院是学校应用性专业综合改革试验田，承载着创新办学模式和人才培养模式的使命。2013年，学院与中国人民大学、南京大学、武汉大学等高校新闻学院一起，入选中宣部、教育部10所部校共建新闻学院试点单位。根据部校共建新闻学院的协议精神，中共安徽省委宣传部和安徽师范大学围绕建设一流新闻学院、培养卓越新闻传播人才这一目标，共建管理体系、共商培养方案、共建核心课程、共建双师队伍、共建实验基地、共建研究平台，投入专项资金，推动新闻与传播学院加速发展成为特色鲜明、国内一流的现代化新闻与传播学院。

　　学院现有教职员工94人，其中专职教师（含实验系列）80人，正高职13人（含高级记者1人），副高职28人，博士（含在读）40人，博士后4人，博士生导师4人，硕士生导师35人，国家级领军人才1人、邹韬奋奖获得者1人、安徽省学术和技术带头人2人，二级教授1人，国务院特殊津贴专家2人，皖江学者特聘教授1人。学院现有新闻学、广告学、摄影、动画、播音与主持艺术、网络与新媒体、航空服务艺术与管理（专升本）等本科专业，以及中韩动画、中英新闻等合作办学形式。其中，新闻学入选国家"双万计划"一流专业建设点，新闻学、动画、摄影等3个专业为安徽省特色专业，播音与主持艺术专业为安徽省综合改革试点专业。拥有新闻传播学、戏剧与影视学2个一级学科硕士学位点，新闻与传播、广播电视2个专业学位硕士点，"文艺、文化与传播"博士招生方向，"马克思主义新闻学与意识形态建设"目录外二级点。获得省级一流专业、省级教学团队、省级教学成果奖、省级"六卓越一拔尖"卓越人才培养创新项目、省重大教改项目、省示范实验实训中心、省校企合作实践教育基地等56项省级质量工程；承担了15项国家社科基金项目（重点1项）、34项省部级科研项目以及30余项应用研究课题和社会服务项目。学院建有安徽省重点人文社科基地——"创意产业发展研究中心"。学院是中网联网络传播专业委员会首批成员单位，拥有首批"安徽省青少年网络素养教育基地"；拥有安徽省网络舆情调查与分析研究中心、安徽师范大学经致科技文化传播有限公司、安徽师范大学"创意港"省级众创空间、"新时代中国国家品牌传播协同创新中心"校级科研平台等。

　　自部校共建新闻学院工作开展以来，学院依托部校共建新闻学院的平台资源，发挥省属重点师范大学学科较为齐全的传统优势，确立"人文与科学并重、理论与实践结合"的目标定位，坚持以学科建设引领专业、学位点建设的发展之路。广大师生围绕马克思主义新闻观和中国特色社会主义新闻传播理论进行系统设计，开展专题研究，撰写了系列论著；打造课程群，组建专门教学团队，建设名师工作坊，编写了系列专业教材；进行创、采、写、摄、编、播、评、管一体化实践，取得了系列创作成果。学院在此基础上，策划了"安徽师范大学传媒视界丛书"，呈现学院在部校共建新闻学院工作中科研、教学、实践方面的成果。

出版"安徽师范大学传媒视界丛书"，旨在充分发挥部校共建新闻学院的平台优势，在新闻传播、品牌传播、媒介文化、艺术传播等研究领域，促进高显示度的标志性成果产生，形成相对明确的学术格局，打造部校共建的安徽师范大学新闻与传播学院学术品牌。我们将以丛书出版为推动，强化团队建设，合理布局研究方向，突出研究的前沿性，将新闻传播学建设成省内一流、国内知名学科；不断提升团队科研能力，凝练研究方向，强化成果的学术水平，将戏剧与影视学建设成目标明晰、特色鲜明的学科；共同打造特色鲜明、优势明显的文化传播学研究团队。

根据学院规划，"安徽师范大学传媒视界丛书"分为学术成果、教材、艺术作品三个子系列。这其中既有学院特聘教授、学术骨干的精品，又有学术新锐、新传学子的力作；既有科研领域的最新探索，又有教学方面的长期思考；既有研究思考的宏观论述，又有实践育人的具体案例；既有隽永文字的深邃详述，又有优秀图片的精彩呈现……综合反映了学院师生在部校共建新闻学院建设中的理论与实务成果。

"安徽师范大学传媒视界丛书"是部校共建新闻学院"十个一工程"中重点项目之一。对此，安徽省委宣传部新闻处给予了充分肯定，并提出了指导性意见。学校领导以及相关职能部门一直关注新传学院的建设与发展，"传媒视界丛书"的出版正是他们的关心的成果之一。新传学院汇聚了新闻传播、品牌传播、艺术传播、文化传播等领域人才，展示出人文与艺术兼容、理论与实践并重的学科发展特色，呈现出"求真、至善、尚美、笃行"的学院文化风貌。学院成立了"安徽师范大学传媒视界丛书"编委会，负责进行丛书的评选等工作。第二届编委会成员由杨柏岭、张师帅、沈正赋、马梅、赵昊、丁云亮、朱晓凯、刘刚、肖叶飞组成。同时，在策划"传媒视界丛书"的过程中，得到学院师生的大力支持，保证了丛书的质量。最后，特别要感谢安徽师范大学出版社领导对这套丛书出版的高度重视，感谢责任编辑为丛书出版所付出的辛勤劳动。我们将以"传媒视界丛书"为抓手，探索学院转型发展之路，以不辜负师生对学院发展的期待。

"安徽师范大学传媒视界丛书"编委会

二〇二〇年十一月

前　言

　　古代的中国在哪里？古代中国是什么模样？如何探寻、触摸、思考与记忆古代的中国……在这一片片景德镇明清民窑青花古瓷碎片上，依稀可见明清时期的中国是绿水青山、鸟飞兽跑、草木依旧，是亭台楼阁、庙堂宗祠、仙台列班，是婴戏挥舞、诗书六艺、点画江山……明清时期的中国曾经是那么模糊、遥远、触不可及，而现今却又是这样的清晰、无距，点点滴滴……残而不失其珍，缺而不失其美。景德镇明清青花古瓷片上的残缺不过是历史的风尘，是文明的碎片，是有心无意、贯通古今，是无心有意，划向心尖……

Preface

　　Where is ancient China? What did ancient China look like? How should ancient China be explored, touched, thought and memorized...? China in Ming and Qing Dynasty can be dimly seen on the pieces of ancient blue and white porcelain fragments from Jingdezhen folk kiln: clear waters and green mountains, flying birds and running animals, flowers and trees as before; pavilions and towels, temples and ancestral halls, gods and goddesses; children's playing and dancing, Chinese classics and calligraphy; paintings of nature...China in Ming and Qing Dynasties used to be so vague, remote and inaccessible, but now it is so clear, not-too-distant and touchable. Those porcelains are fragmentary but not losing its value, missing but not losing its beauty. The incompleteness on the ancient blue and white porcelain chips of Jingdezhen in Ming and Qing Dynasties is only the dust of history and the fragments of civilization. Intentionally or unintentionally, it connects the past and the present. Intentionally or unintentionally, it goes to the heart.

目　录

山 高 水 长

High Mountains and Long Rivers

乐　山

　　山，厚德载物，经受着严寒酷暑、狂风暴雨、雷电交加，与冰雪为侣，与河流作伴，养育着参天大树、名花小草、鸟兽昆虫，孕育了人生的悲与欢、苦与乐。它象征着民族志气、理想，象征着人们顽强的意志和不屈不挠、勇于登攀的精神。

Enjoying the Mountains

　　Mountains are loads of virtue. Suffering severe cold and hot weather, strong wind and heavy storms, thunder and lightning, snow and ice, streams and rivers, they raise towering trees, beautiful flowers and soft grass, birds, animals and insects, and breed the sorrow and joy of life at the same time. They represent national aspiration and ideals, symbolize people's firm eyes and tenacious will, and signify people's spirit of perseverance and courage.

灵　芝

灵芝功效奇绝，古朴典雅。古人，把菌盖的环形轮纹，称做"瑞征"或"庆云"，视为吉祥如意、祥瑞长寿的象征，所以灵芝又有"仙草""瑞草"之称。

Ganoderma Lucidum

Ganoderma lucidum is extraordinary in effect as well as looks plain and elegant. Ancient people called the annular wheel pattern of the its pileus "signal of auspice" or "joyous clouds" as a symbol of good luck and longevity. Ganoderma lucidum was also called "magic herb" or "auspicious herb".

莲

　　莲，出污泥而不染，人们认为是洁身自好、不同流合污的高尚品德的象征，把莲喻为君子，圣洁的形象。

Lotus

　　Lotus come out of sludge without being stained. People regard lotus as symbols of noble personality of self-purification. Lotus also metaphorically represents gentlemen and holy images.

柳

柳是春天的使者，又谐音"留"，象征不舍的别离，成为离情、思人、思乡之情的代表。

Willow

Willow is the messenger of spring. It is homophonic to Chinese character "liu" symbolizing the inseparable feeling of departure, standing for meaning of leaving and homesickness.

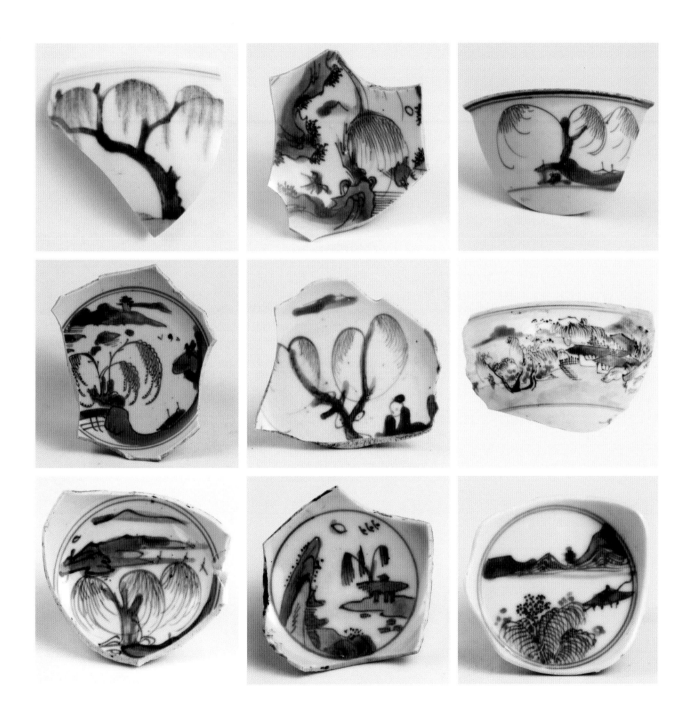

龙

龙是古代传说中一种有鳞有须能兴云作雨的神异动物。

龙是中华文化里的主要图腾、主要象征。

龙是封建时代中国帝王的象征。

Dragon

Dragon is a kind of miracle animal with scales and palpi in ancient legends, which is able to bring clouds and fall rain.

Dragon is the main totem and symbol in Chinese culture. It is also Chinese emperor' symbol in feudal times.

The dragon is the symbol of Chinese emperors in feudal times.

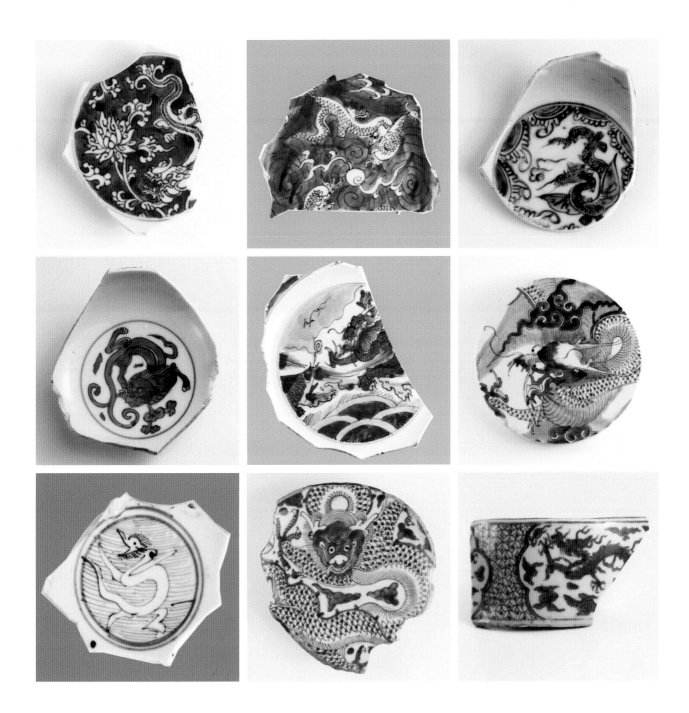

凤　凰

凤凰，中国古代传说中的百鸟之王，与"龙"同为汉民族图腾。

凤凰与麒麟一样是雌雄统称，雄为"凤"，雌为"凰"，总称为"凤凰"，象征祥瑞。

Phoenix

As the king of birds in ancient Chinese legends, like dragon, phoenix is the totem in Han nationality.

Phoenix, like kylin, is a collective name for the male and female. The male phoenix is called "Feng" and the female is called "Huang", symbolizing auspiciousness.

麒　麟

麒麟，古代传说的一种仁兽、瑞兽，是吉祥神宠，主太平、长寿、祥瑞。它外形像鹿，头上有角，全身有鳞甲，尾像牛尾。麒麟造型集合了人们所珍爱的动物全部优点，充分体现了中国人的"集美"思想。

Kylin

Kylin is a kind of benevolent and auspicious beast in ancient legends. It symbolizes peace, longevity and auspiciousness. It looks like a deer with horns on its head, scales all over its body, and tails like tails of cattle. The shape of Kylin concentrates all the advantages of the animals that people cherish, which fully embodies the Chinese thought of "collecting beauty".

狮　子

狮子，我国民俗文化中常见的吉祥神兽，是智慧和力量的化身，代表英勇、王权和保护力，象征地位、尊严、吉祥、平安。

Lion

A lion, commonly seen as an auspicious sacred animal in Chinese folk culture, is the embodiment of wisdom and strength. It also represents bravery, kingship and protection as a symbol of status, dignity, auspiciousness and peace.

鹿

鹿是美丽的。人们尤其喜爱鹿天性中蕴含的善良、柔美、内敛气质。

"鹿"与"禄"谐音，象征着富裕，生财有"鹿"。

Deer

Deer is People especially like the kind, gentle and restrained temperament in deer's nature.

The homonym of "deer" and "lu" symbolizes wealth and "deer" is the source of wealth.

马

　　马是刚健、明亮、热烈、高昂、升腾、饱满、昌盛、发达的代名词，代表中华民族自古以来所崇尚的奋斗不止、自强不息、进取向上的民族精神。

　　马又是能力、圣贤、人才、有作为的象征，古人常常以"千里马"来比拟有才能的人。

Horse

Horse is a symbol of vigor, brightness, enthusiasm, high-spiritedness, rising, fullness, prosperity and advancement. It represents the national spinit of unremitting struggling and improvement.

Horse is also a symbol of ability, sage, talent and achievement. The smart and talented people are often compared with "fiery steeds" by ancient people.

鹰

鹰，是原始社会的图腾崇拜，是神的化身，因此，被蒙上了神秘的色彩，奉为神鸟、天鸟、神鹰。在古代军事上，鹰象征"战神"。

Eagle

Eagle, is totem worship in primitive society. It is the incarnation of God. Covered with mysterious color, eagles are regarded as divine birds, birds of heaven and holy eagles. In ancient times, the eagle symbolized "the God of war".

兔　子

古书《瑞应图》记载："赤兔大瑞，白兔中瑞。"古时人们如发现白兔，多要载歌载舞献给朝廷，显示君主贤明、海内大治。古代的野生兔子毛色多为灰褐色，白兔极为稀少，被认为是一种变异现象，因而被古人认为是"中瑞"，献给皇上。

Rabbit

The ancient book *Ruiyingtu*: "Red Rabbit stands for great auspiciousness, white Rabbit moderate auspiciousness." In ancient times, when white rabbits were found, they were mostly dedicated to the court by singing and dancing, which showed the emperor's wisdom and stability of the country. The color of wild rabbits in old times was regarded as mostly gray brown, and white rabbits were rare, which was a phenomenon of mutation. Therefore, white rabbits were regarded as " moderate auspiciousness " by the ancients and dedicated to the emperor.

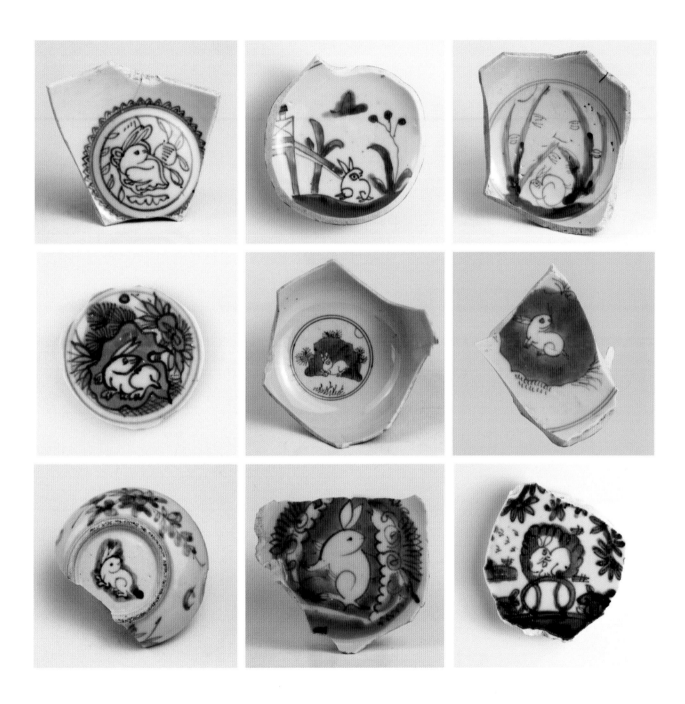

爱情鸟

爱情鸟，代表鸟类世界忠贞不二的爱情。

千百年来，爱情鸟一直是夫妻和睦相处、相亲相爱的美好象征，也是中国文艺作品中坚贞不移的纯洁爱情的化身，备受赞颂。

Love Bird

Love bird, stands for the faithful Love in the Bird World.

For thousands of years, love bird has been a beautiful sign of harmonious coexistence and mutual love. It is also a highly praised personification of the unshakable pure love in Chinese literary works.

锦　鸡

　　锦鸡是一种雉科动物，是学名白腹锦鸡、红腹锦鸡的统称。它分布在陕西、西藏、四川、贵州、云南、广西等地，属国家二级保护动物。

Golden Pheasant

Golden pheasant is a pheasant, a general term for white-bellied and red-bellied pheasants, They distribute in Shanxi (Shangluo), Tibet, Sichuan, Guizhou, Yunnan, Guangxi and other places. They second-class national protected animals.

鱼

从远古狩猎、采集时代起，鱼一直与人类生活密切相关。鱼繁殖力强，生长迅速，象征着家族兴旺、人丁众多。

"鱼"与"余"谐音，象征着富贵。人们也习惯用"如鱼得水"描写生活和谐美满、幸福自在。

Fish

From the time of hunting and collecting in ancient times, fish has been closely related to human life. It has strong reproductive capacity and grows rapidly, which symbolizes the prosperity of the family and the large number of people.

"Fish" and "Yu" are homophonic, which symbolizes wealth. Phrase "Like a fish getting water" describes life in harmony, happiness and ease

虾

虾，身躯弯弯，却顺畅自如，一节比一节高，象征遇事圆满顺畅、节节高升、官运亨通。

Shrimp

Shrimp body is bending, but smooth and free in swimming. sections of its body is getting higher and higher one by one, symbolizing success in doing things, rising in status and prosperity in official fortune.

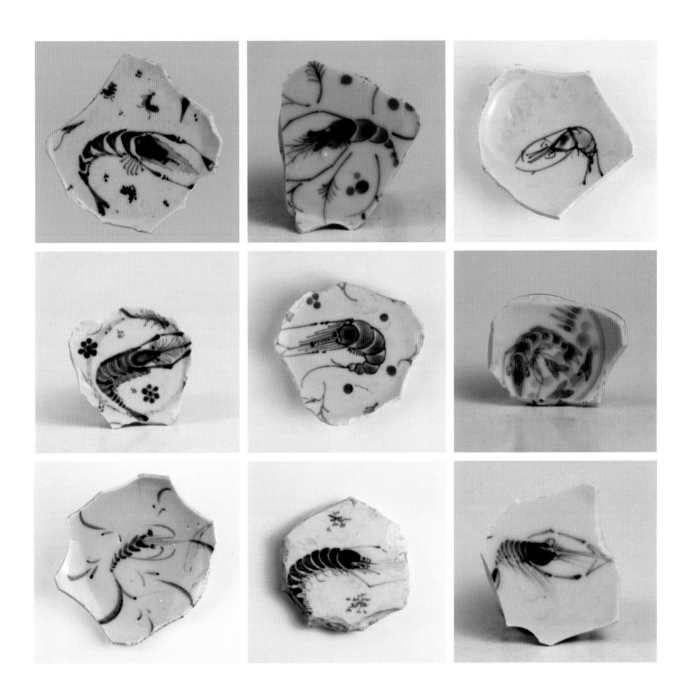

蟹

蟹有八条腿横行，"八"谐音"发"，寓意发财，象征着八面来财、财运亨通；八只脚落在地上，寓意着人四平八稳，步步高升。螃蟹煮熟后成红色，寓意鸿运当头、好运连连。

蟹自古就寓意解元，也就是第一。蟹身成椭圆形，有着王者之风，象征着才华横溢、金榜题名。

Crab

Crab runs sideway with its eight legs. "Eight" and "fa" are homophonic, indicating making a fortune and symbolizing prosperity of all sources. Eight feet land on the ground, implying that people are stable and steadily rise to higher level. When the crab is cooked, it turns red, which means good luck.

Since ancient times, crabs have implied the scholar who won the first place in provincial imperial examinations. Crabs are oval in shape and have the style of king, which symbolizes the brilliance and gold placard nomination.

草　虫

《草虫》，出自《诗经·国风》，是思情的诗歌，思情怀之作，表达了对钟爱之人的思念，亦有"大夫归心召公说""室家思念南仲说""托男女情以写君臣念说"等。

Katydid

Katydid, originated from the Book of *Songs*, is a poem of sentiment, a piece of works of memorizing beloved person.

There are also interpretation as "Dafu Rui Liangfu shows loyalty to Zhaogong Jishi", "Wife misses husband Nanzhong", "Relationship between monarchs and ministers is covered with love between men and women" and so on.

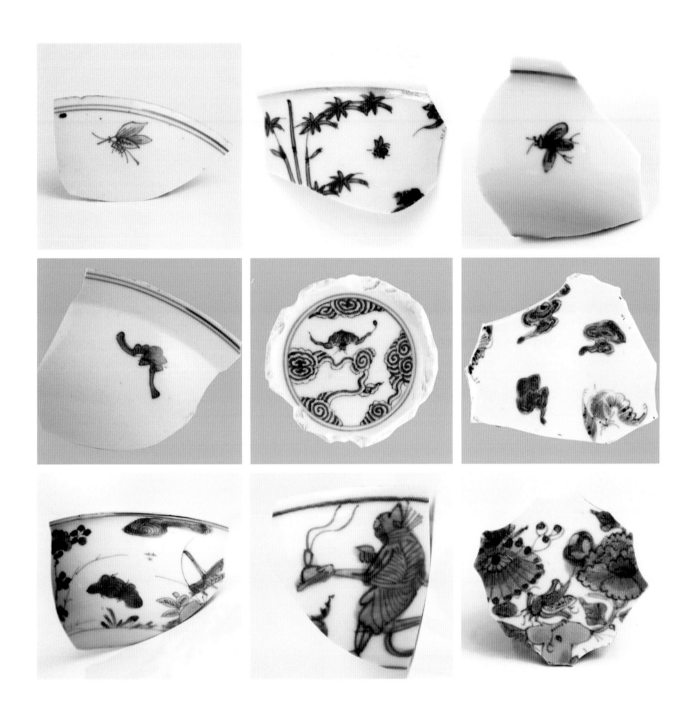

上善若水

　　道德经："上善若水，水善利万物而不争，处众人之所恶，故几于道。"即做人应如水，水滋润万物，不与万物争高下，这样的品格才最接近道。

Great Virtue Is Like Water

The Book of *Tao and Teh*: "Good virture is like water", which has a long history and never ceases to grow.

"Water is closely similar to Tao because it benefits all things but does not contend, and stays in places people dislike." That is to say, a man should be like water, which moistens all things but does not compete with others. character like this is the closest to Tao.

宗 教 宗 族
Religion and Family

道　教

　　道教继承华夏民族古代原始宗教之血脉，从敬天祭祖到殷商天神崇拜，从春秋战国黄老道家到秦汉神仙方术以及东汉"五斗米道"与"太平道"一路走来。

　　道教以尊"道"为最高信仰，而"道"的尊高和伟大最高体现就是"德"，"道"与"德"构成其教理核心内容。

Taoism

　　Inheriting the ancient primitive religions of the Chinese nation, Taoism originated from memorial service of heaven and ancestors to worship of gods in Yin and Shang Dynasties. It deveiops with Taoism of Huangdi and Laozi in Spring and Autumn period and Warring States Period to immortal Arts and folk beliefs in Qin and Han Dynasties, and the " Five Pecks of Rice Taoism" and "Great Fairness Taoism" in Eastern Han Dynasty.

　　Respect for "Tao" is the highest belief of Taoism, and the highest expression of the dignity and greatness of Tao is "virtue". "Tao" and "virtue" constitute the core content of its doctrine.

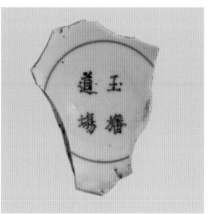

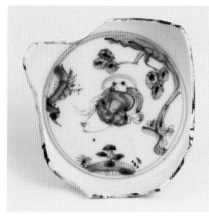

太极八卦

在《周易》中，“太极”是派生万物的本原。《周易》中的八种基本图形，主要象征天、地、雷、风、水、火、山、泽八种自然现象。

Taiji–Bagua

In *Zhouyi*, "Tai Chi" is the origin of all things derived. The eight basic figures in *Zhouyi* symbolize the eight natural phenomena of heaven, earth, thunder, wind, water, fire, mountains and Ze.

刘伶醉酒

刘伶，魏晋时沛国（今安徽淮北市濉溪县）人，"竹林七贤"之一。嗜酒不羁，被称为醉侯、酒仙。

刘伶作《酒德颂》，宣扬老庄思想和纵酒放诞之情趣，反映了魏晋名士崇尚玄虚、消极颓废的心态，也表现出对"名教"礼法的蔑视及对自然的向往，透露出对个性独立和精神自由的追求！面对残酷的现实，他无力反抗，唯有酒才能消除内心的痛苦和无奈的惆怅。

Liu Ling's Intoxication

Liu Ling, known as drunken marquis, alcoholic Immortals for his liquor addiction, lived in Wei and Jin Dynasties in Kingdom of Pei (now Suixi County, Huaibei City, Anhui Province) and was one member of the "The Seven Sages of the Bamboo Grove".

His "Ode to Wine Virtue" advocates Lao Zi and Zhuang Zi's thought and indulgence in drinking. It reflects absurdity-pursuit and negative attitude of the celebrities in Wei and Jin Dynasties, and shows contempt for the etiquette of "Famous Religion" and yearning for nature as well, indicating his pursuit of individual independence and spiritual freedom. Faced with the cruel reality, is was unable to resist, and only wine can eliminate the inner pain and helpless melancholy.

佛　教

　　"佛教"的"佛"，意思是"觉者"。它重视人类心灵的觉悟和道德的进步，主张众生平等，认为有生皆苦，以超脱生死为理想境界。佛教认为，其修习的目的在于发现生命和宇宙的真相，超越生死和苦，断尽一切烦恼，以此得到解脱。

Buddhism

　　Buddha, which means "awakened person", attaches importance to the progress of morality and consciousness of human mind. It advocates the equality of all living beings and the bitterness of lifetime, desiring for the ideal state of transcending life and death. Buddha thinks the purpose of Buddhist practice is to discover the truth of life and the universe, transcend life and death and suffering, cut off all worries and be free from them.

罗　汉

罗汉，阿罗汉的简称，意译"应供"，即当受众生供养。在小乘佛教中，罗汉是佛陀得法弟子修成正果的最高果位。

罗汉像因无经典仪轨依据，会随各代的艺术家来创作表现。他通常是剃发出家的比丘形像，身着僧衣，简朴清净，姿态不拘，随意自在，反映了现实中清修梵行、睿智安祥的高僧德性。

Luohan

Arhat, short for Arahant, paraphrase "shall provide", that is, when the audience is born to provide support. In Theravada Buddhism, Arhat is the highest attainment position for the Buddha's disciples to cultivate righteousness.

Since there is no basis for classical rituals, Luohan statues vary with the creation of artists in different generations. Usually it is the image of a Bhiksu dressed in a monk's clothes, simple and pure, free and easy, reflecting the virtue of a wise and peaceful monk who practices Buddhism in reality.

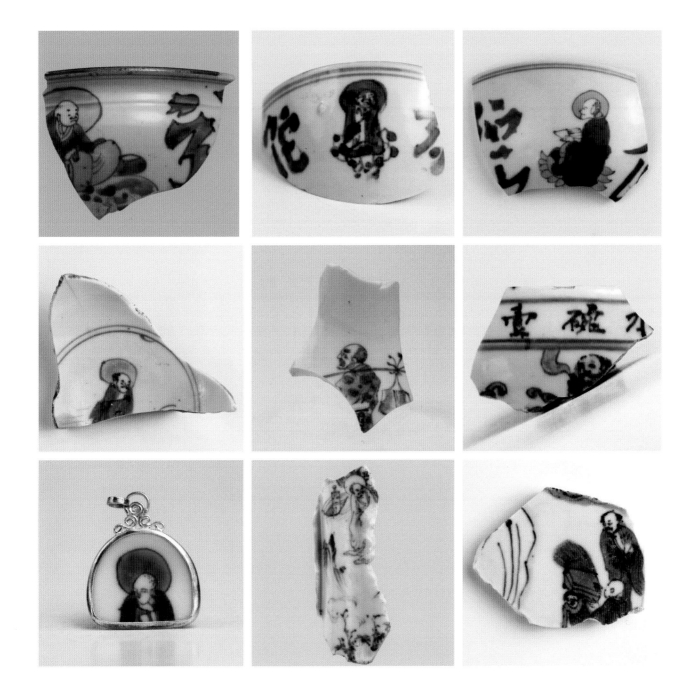

十字金刚杵

十字金刚杵又称羯磨杵，系古印度一种兵器，由两个金刚杵相交叉构成"十"字形得名，后演变为密宗法器：坚固锋利，断烦恼，除恶魔，可消除自身一切罪障……

Cruciform Vajra

Cruciform vajra is also known as karma pestle, an ancient Indian weapon that later evolved into a Tantric sacred instrument: firm, sharp, trouble-free and devil-free. which can eliminate all their own obstacles. It deserves its name for shape of "十" by the intersection of two diamond pestles.

儒　教

儒教又称"孔教""圣教""礼教"或"先王之教"。它是以孔子为先师，"祖述尧舜，宪章文武"，倡导王道德治、尊王攘夷和上下秩序的道德文化精髓。

Confucianism

Confucianism is also known as "Confucian Religion" "Sacred Religion" "Ritual Religion" or "The Religion of the Ancient Kings". With Confucius as the forerunner and sage as the deity, Confucianism follows ideas of Yao and Shun, obeys rules of King Wen and King Wu of Zhou Dynasty. It advocates the state management by the rule of morality, respect for the king and banishment for the barbarians, and maintenance of the status order.

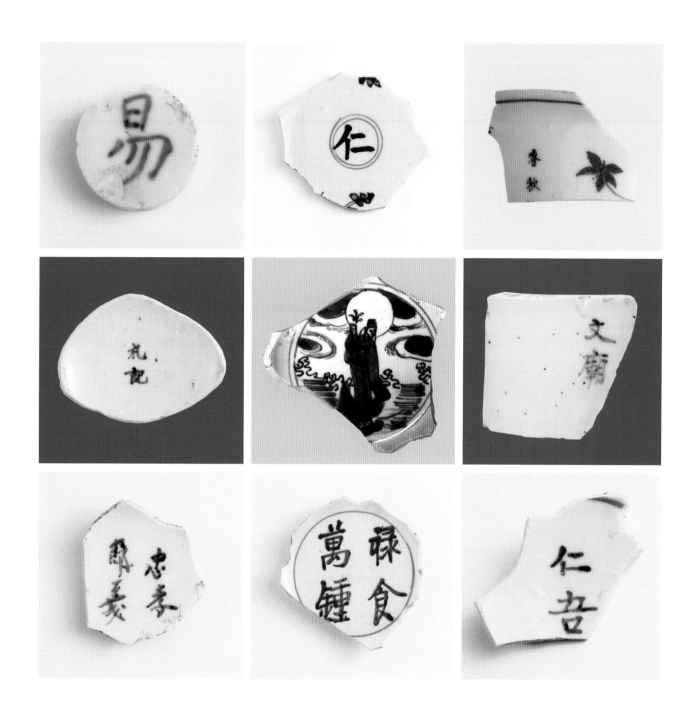

宗族宗祠

宗族，谓同宗同族之人。一个宗族通常表现为一个姓氏，并构成共同的居住空间，包括很多家庭。

宗祠，即祠堂或家庙，旧时同族子孙供奉并祭祀祖先的处所。

Clan Ancestral Hall

Clan means people of the same clan. A clan is usually expressed as a surname and constitutes a common living space, including many families.

Ancestral halls, namely ancestral halls or family temples, were used to worship and worship their ancestors by descendants of the same race.

祭　祀

祭祀是一种源于天地自然乃至万物和谐共生的信仰活动与理念。追求的是人心理认知思维意义上的感悟、对话与沟通，实现天地万物人神和谐共生的信仰欲念。

Sacrifice

Sacrifice offering is a kind of belief activity and idea originated from the harmonious coexistence of heaven,earth,nature and all things. What we pursue is the perception, dialogue and communication in the sense of human psychological cognitive thinking, so as to realize the belief desire of harmonious coexistence of human beings and gods.

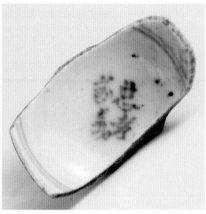
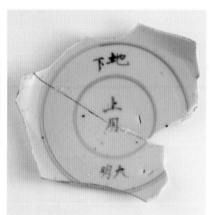

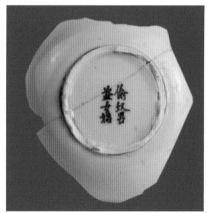

大　房

　　唐朝世家大族各支以房划分，用始祖的官名、爵名或封地称其房，长次之间并有大房、小房、二房、三房、四房、五房等分别。后世家族以大房称长房。

A Wife in Main House

　　Each branch of big families in Tang Dynasty is divided into houses, which are named by the official name, title or fief of the ancestors. There are main house, first house, second house, third house, fourth house, and fifth house etc. Families of later generations called elder house by main house

庙 堂 江 湖
Imperial Court and Civilian Society

朝堂议政

汉代王充《论衡·效力》载:"治书定簿,佐史之力也;论道议政,贤儒之力也。"

宋朝韩元吉《读〈管子〉》:"则仲之与桓公平日谋国议政者,其亦详矣。"

《清史稿·太宗纪二》载:"(崇德二年夏四月)丁酉,命固山其子尼堪、罗托、博洛等预议国政。增置每旗议政大臣三人,集群臣谕之曰向者议政大臣额少……今特择尔等置之议政之列,当以民生休戚为念,慎毋怠惰,有负朝廷。"

Court Administration

On Fairness and Power by Wangchong of Han dynasty: "The power of assisting officials is to compile books; and the power of virtuous scholars is to comment on politics and morality".

Readings on Guanzi by Han Yuanji of Song dynasty: "It is detailed about Guan Zhong and King Huan's comment on political affairs"~

History of the Qing Dynasty· Recording of Taizong II: "In the year of Ding You (April of Summer days, 2nd year of Chongde), Nikan, Luotuo, Bolo etc. were ordered to discuss state affairs previously. Three more ministers were selected from each Qi(equals to county), and the ministers were gathered together to be told: The number of Ministers who comment on state affairs was too few in the past…… Today you all are selected here, so you should take the people's livelihood as your concern, be careful not to be lazy and let us down. "

六　艺

　　六艺，中国周朝的贵族教育体系，开始于公元前1046年的周王朝，周王官学要求学生掌握的六种基本才能：礼、乐、射、御、书、数。出自《周礼·保氏》："养国子以道，乃教之六艺：一曰五礼，二曰六乐，三曰五射，四曰五御，五曰六书，六曰九数。"这就是所说的"通五经贯六艺"的"六艺"。

Six Arts

　　The aristocratic education system in China began in the Zhou Dynasty in 1046 B.C. The official schools of the Zhou Dynasty required students to master six basic abilities: ritual, music, archery, carriage-driving, calligraphy and mathematics, which came from *ZhouLi Baoshi*: "Cultivating students in Imperial College by Tao, and teaching them with the six arts: the first one is Five Rituals, the second one is Six pieces of Music, the third one is Five Shooting techniques, the fourth one is five ways of carriage-driving, and the five one is six forms of calligraphy, the sixth one is nine conceptions in mathematics." This is the so-called "six arts" in "understanding the five classics and being skillful in six arts"

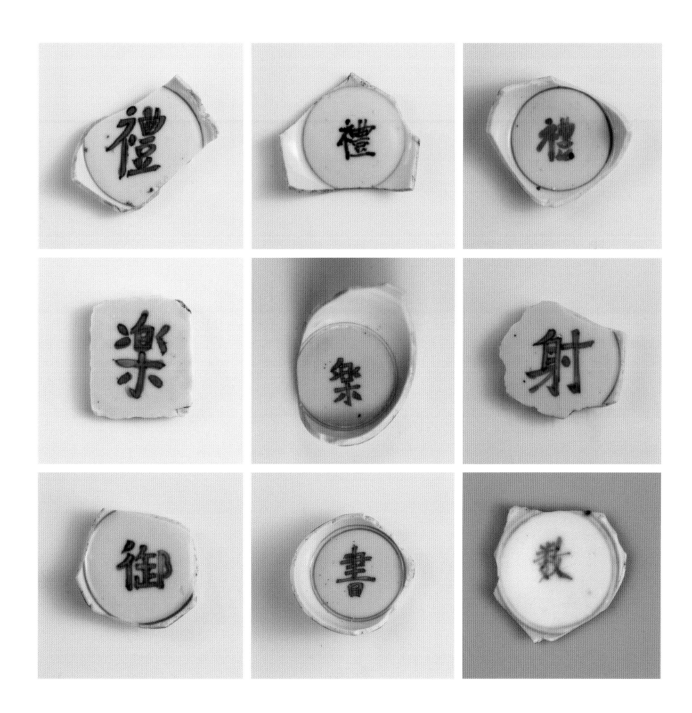

博古纹

博古纹是装饰中一种典型的纹样。博古即古代器物，由《宣和博古图》一书得名。此书著录当时皇室在宣和殿所藏商至唐代铜器839件，集宋代所藏青铜器之大成，故而得名"博古"。

Bogu Patterns

Bogu Patterns is a typical pattern in decoration. Bogu refers to ancient artifacts, named after the book of *Xuanhe Bogu Pictures*, which described 839 bronze wares from Shang Dynasty to Tang Dynasty in Xuanhe Palace. Those were the most collections of bronze wares in Song Dynasty, thus contributed to the name Bogu.

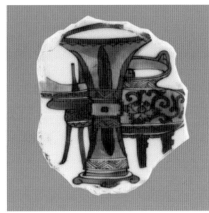

科　举

　　科举，中国古代通过考试选拔官吏的制度。由于采用分科取士的办法，所以叫做科举。 科举打破血缘世袭和世族的垄断，"朝为田舍郎，暮登天子堂"，使社会中下层有能力的读书人可以获得施展才智的机会。科举制在中国前后经历一千三百余年，成为世界延续时间最长的选拔人才的办法。

Imperial Examination

　　Imperial Examination is a system of selecting officials through examinations in ancient China. It is called imperial examination because it adopts the method of selecting intellectuals from different academic fields. Imperial Examination breaks the monopoly of heredity and descendants, and "A farmer in the morning and an official in the court in the evening". The capable personnel in the middle and lower classes of society can get the opportunity to display their talents. The imperial examination system has experienced more than 1,300 years in China and has become the longest way to select talents in the world.

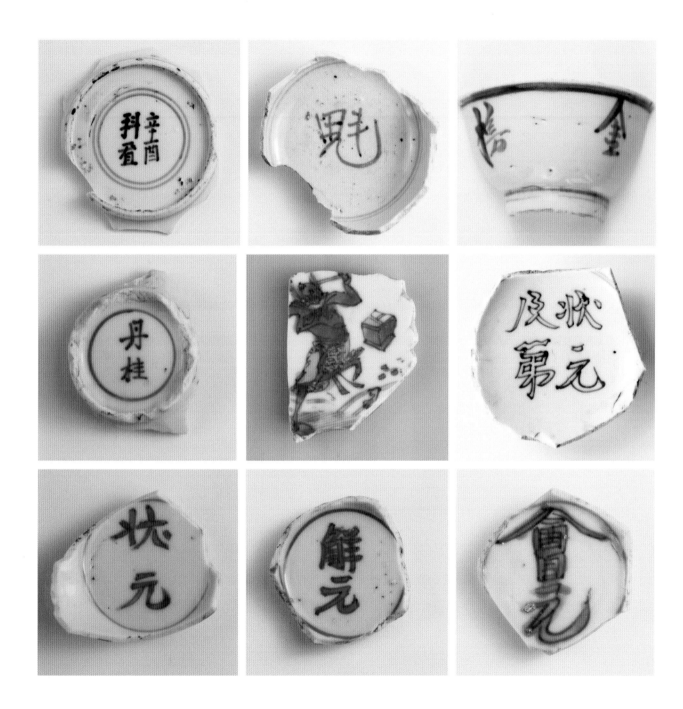

状元游街

金榜题名和状元游街，是古代科场举子殿试后梦寐以求的事。

皇帝在金銮殿传胪唱名，钦点状元、榜眼、探花和进士后，状元领诸进士拜谢皇恩后，到长安左门外观看张贴金榜及回家的过程。

Champion Parade

Name on the passing list of imperial examination and champion parade are the dreams of ancient candidates for the imperial examinations.

After the emperor announced their names in the Jin Luan Temple and appointed the first prize, the second prize, the third prize and the other scholars, the champion led all the scholars to thank the emperor for his graciousness and went to the left gate of Chang'an street to see the process of posting the name list and returning home.

深　闺

深闺，旧时指富贵人家的女子所住的闺房。

在中国的传统文化中，未婚女子的住所称作"闺房"。它一般在住所较隐蔽的位置，是青春少女坐卧起居、修炼女红、研习诗书礼仪的地方。

Boudoir

Boudoir refers to the room where the rich woman lives.

In traditional Chinese culture, unmarried women's residence is called "boudoir". It often located in the most concealed place in the family, where young girls live, sleep, practice needlework and study classics and etiquette.

婴戏图

婴戏图，中国人物画的一种，以描绘儿童游戏为主，表现童真为主要目的，画面丰富，形态有趣，象征着多子多福，生活美满。

婴戏图最早出现在唐代长沙窑瓷器上，宋代进入了黄金期，成为中国绘画中极受欢迎的画类。

Children Playing Pictures

It is one of the Chinese figure paintings depicting children's games. The main purpose is to show childlike innocence. The pictures are rich and the forms are interesting.

Children Playing Pictures first appeared on the porcelains of Changsha kiln in Tang Dynasty, and entered the golden age in Song Dynasty. It became a very popular kind of painting in Chinese paintings, symbolizing many children, many blessings and happy life.

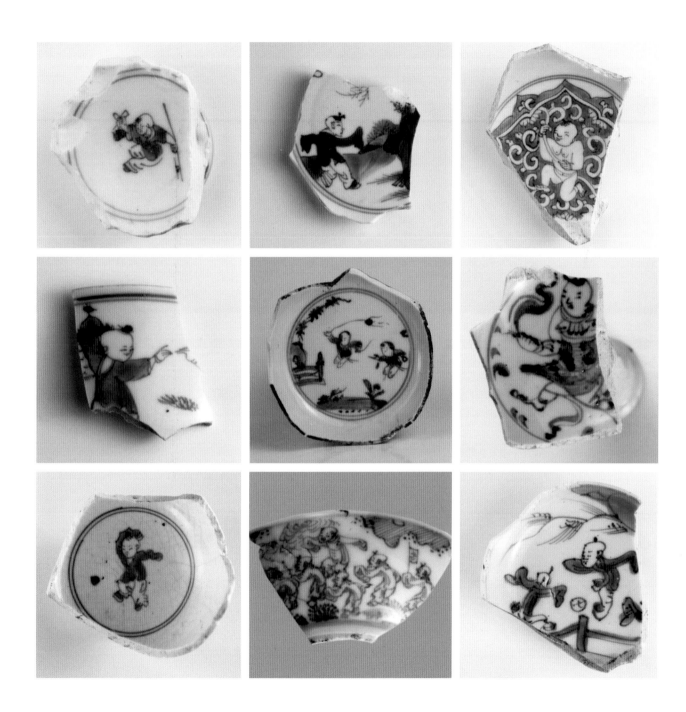

行　旅

　　行旅，往来的旅客，远行的人。《汉语大词典》对其释义为：1.旅客。《孟子·梁惠王上》："商贾皆欲藏于王之市，行旅皆欲出于王之涂"。唐代孟浩然《夜渡湘水》诗："行侣时相问，浔阳何处边？"《明史·宦官传二·陈奉》："每讬巡历，鞭笞官吏，剽劫行旅。"郭小川《春暖花开》诗："柳条扬手，为田野招徕行旅"。2.出行；旅行。南朝宋谢瞻《答灵运》诗："叹彼行旅艰，深兹眷言情。"3.即行李。

Travel

　　Passengers coming and going, people traveling far. *Chiese Ditiorary* explams "travel"as 1. Passengers. "Mencius, King Liang Hui": "Businessmen all want to trade in the market of our kingdom, and travelers all want to come in or out of our kingdom too. Meng Haoran's poem in Tang Dynasty "Crossing Xiang River at Night": "Travelers ask frequently where Xunyang is？" "History of the Ming Dynasty, Eunuch Biography II. Chen Feng": "Very often he was in the name of inspection tour to whip officials and rob passengers." Guo Xiaochuan's poem "Spring Flowers": "Wickers wave to welcome travelers for the land"~2. Outgoing; travel. Song Xiezhan's poem in Southern Dynasties "Answering Lingyun": "Sigh at the difficulty of traveling soon, and appreciate the sentiment deeply now." 3. Baggage.

访　友

关于"友"字，《说文解字》云："友，同志为友。"《礼记·儒行》载："儒有合志同方，营道同术。并立则乐，相下不厌。久不相见，闻流言不信。其行本方立义，同而进，不同而退。其交友有如此者。"

Friends Visit

Origin of Chinese Characters: "People with same interests are Friends" ~ "*Rites · Principles of Confucians*" said: Confucians are people having same interests and principles, pursuing moral principles with same methods, being happy with people of similar social status, never resenting others of higher or lower position, never believing in rumors even no seeing each other for a long time, their behavior going upright, advancing with people of same moral principles while retreating with people of different ones. That's their attitudes of making friends.

祝　寿

祝寿，庆祝诞辰。一般以晚辈出面，表示对长辈孝敬。礼物多是衣料、鞋袜、鸡公、酒、寿桃（笑包）、寿面（面条），也有赠送匾额的。寿宴头道菜一定是寿面，取寿延绵长之意。

Birthday Congratulations

Birthday congratulations means. Celebrating the birthday.

To live a longevity, younger generation are usually willing to show filial piety to their older. Gifts are mostly clothing, footwear, cocks, liquid, peaches (blossoming steamed bun), longevity noodles (noodles), and some have plaques as gifts. The first dish of birthday banquet must be longevity noodles for the symbol of long lives.

孙思邈医虎

典故孙思邈医虎，又称虎守杏林，已有1400多年历史，精研医学并兼通佛典，被誉为"药王"的唐代著名医学家孙思邈晚年曾云游于邱县。此间，有虎伏跪求医，孙思邈首创"虎撑"治愈金簪卡喉之疾。虎有灵性，后不复危害人畜，并感恩为药王守护杏林，充当坐骑。

Sun Simiao's Treatment on A Tiger

Also known as tiger guarding apricot forest, the allusion has a history of more than 1400 years. Sun Simiao, a famous physician in Tang Dynasty, known as the "King of Medicine", was good at medicine and Buddhist scripture, and traveled in county Qiu in his later years. There is a tiger knelt to seek medical treatment. Sun Simiao pioneered the "tiger support" to cure the throat disease stuck by hairpins. The tiger has spirituality, so no longer harm people and livestock, and thank for medicine king by guarding the apricot forest and acting as the mount.

琴高乘鲤图

《列仙传》载：琴高为战国时赵人，善鼓琴，曾为宋康王舍人，有长生之术，后遁入涿水中取龙子，临行与诸弟子约期相见，嘱在河旁设祠堂，结齐等候他复出。此图表现琴高辞别众弟子乘鲤而去的情景。

Picture of Qin Gao Riding the Carp

Biography of All Gods said: Qin Gao was a native of Zhao during the Warring States Period, who was good at playing piano. He was once a follower of King Kang of Song Dynasty and had the skill of living forever. Later he dived into Zhuoshui River to fetch baby dragon. He made an appointment with his disciples and ordered them to set up an ancestral hall near the River and wait for his return. This picture shows the scene of Qin Gao leaving his disciple by carp.

渔歌子

张志和的《渔歌子》云："西塞山前白鹭飞，桃花流水鳜鱼肥，青箬笠，绿蓑衣，斜风细雨不须归。"

张志和，唐代诗人，字子同，号烟波钓徒、玄真子。少年成名，平步青云，有感于宦海风波和人生无常，弃官归隐黟县赤山镇（今祁门县祁山镇）石山坞，浪迹江湖，渔樵为乐。

Fishermen's Songs

Zhang Zhihe's *Fishing Songs* says: "The egret flies in front of the Xisai Mountain, the peach blossoms the flowing water. Mandarin fish are fat. The green bamboo hat, the green coir raincoat, and the slanting wind and drizzle do not need to return."

Zhang Zhihe, a poet in the Tang Dynasty, with the same characters, named Yanbo Diaozui, Xuan Zhenzi. He became famous when he was young, and he felt a sense of the turmoil and impermanence of life. Abandoned his officials and returned to Shishanwu, Chishan Town, Yixian County (now Qishan Town, Qimen County).

渡　人

朱德元帅有首《游七屋岩》诗，末云："开心才见胆，破腹任人钻。腹中天地阔，常有渡人船。"

渡人就是把人从烦恼的此岸引领到清净的彼岸；自渡，就是让自己借智慧之力解脱烦恼。要想渡人，必须先自渡。至于如何自渡，先必须认识自己烦恼的是什么，要认识自己。

Ferryman

The poem written by Zhu De called *Visiting the Qixing Cliff asys*. "Being happy to see the courage; breaking the abdomen for others to burrow. There are breadth and width in the abdomen; with ferry boats in it often."

Ferrying others is to lead people from the troubled shore to the trouble-free shore; ferrying ourselves is to free us from troubles with the help of wisdom. If we want to ferry people, we must first ferry ourselves. As for how to ferry ourselves, we must know what our trouble is as well as ourselves first.

诚　信

　　《礼记·祭统》有云是故贤者之祭也，致其诚信，与其忠敬。诚信，属道德范畴，是人的第二个"身份证"，在日常行为中，是诚实和信用的综合表现，即待人处事真诚、老实、讲信誉，言必信、行必果，一言九鼎，一诺千金。如，经商者讲究诚信为本。

Sincerity

　　The Book of *Rites · Sacrifice System* says: The reasons for the old sages to offer sacrifices are showing their honesty, loyalty and worship. Honesty belongs to the category of morality and is the second "ID card" of human beings. In daily activities, it is a comprehensive manifestation of honesty and credit: treating people with sincerity, honesty, prestige, trustworthiness and deeds, and keeping promise. For example,business people play attention to honesty.

长坂坡

赵云，三国常山真定（今河北正定）人，字子龙。初从公孙瓒，后归刘备。

曹操取荆州，刘备败于当阳长坂。赵云力战救护甘夫人和刘禅。赵云怀抱后主，单枪匹马，直破重围，七进七出，砍倒大旗两面，夺槊三条，前后枪刺剑砍，杀死曹营战将五十余员，被誉为"一身都是胆"。

Changban Slope

Zhao Yun, a native of Zhengding (now Zhengding, Hebei Province) in Changshan during the time of Three Kingdoms, has another name Zilong. Served for Gongsun Zan at first then for Liu Bei finally.

Cao Cao invaded Jingzhou and Liu Bei was defeated in Changban, Dangyang. Zhao Yun fought to rescue Liu Bei's wife Mrs. Gan and his son Liu Chan. Zhao Yun embraced the queen, single-handedly, broke through the encirclement, seven in and seven out, cut down two flags and seized three long spears, and killed more than fifty warriors in Cao Cao's army with spear and sword. He was known as "all is courage".

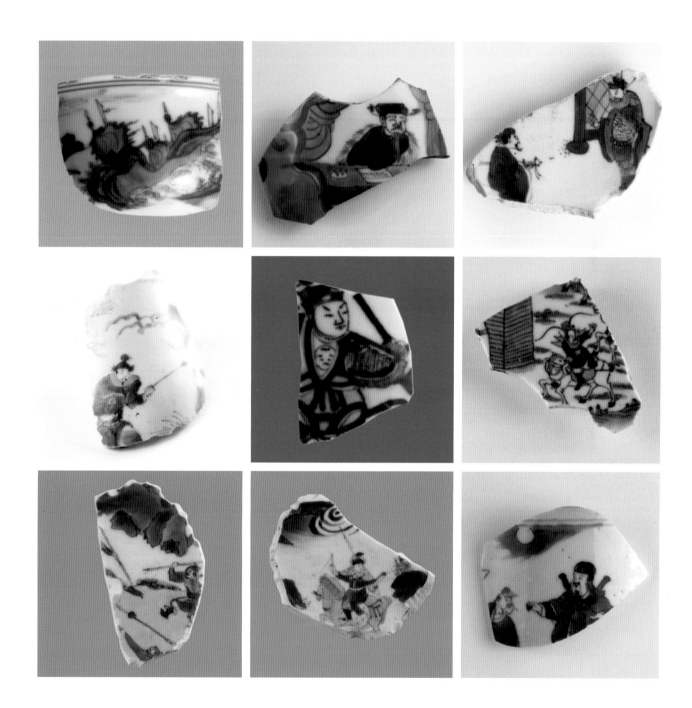

报　捷

报捷指报告胜利的消息。

Success Announcement

Success Announcement is a good news from the ancients.

木兰围场

　　承德皇家猎苑——木兰围场，位于河北东北部。这里自古以来就是一处水草丰美、禽兽繁衍的草原，也是清代皇帝举行"木兰秋狝"之所。公元1681年清帝康熙为锻炼军队，在这里开辟了一万多平方千米的狩猎场。每年秋季，这里都举行一次军事色彩浓厚的狩猎活动，史称"木兰秋狝"。在清代康熙到嘉庆的一百四十多年里，就在这里举行木兰秋狝一百零五次。

Mulan Paddock

　　Chengde Royal Hunting Garden, Mulan Paddock, is located in the northeast of Hebei , Since ancient times, it has been a grassland with abundant water, grass, birds and animals. Qing Emperor held "Mulan Autumn Hunting" here. In 1681, Emperor Kangxi of the Qing Dynasty opened a hunting ground of more than 10,000 square kilometers to train the army. Every autumn, there was a hunting activity with strong military colour, historically known as "Mulan Autumn Hunting". During the 140 years from Kangxi to Jiaqing in the Qing Dynasty, there were 105 Mulan Autumn Hunting held here.

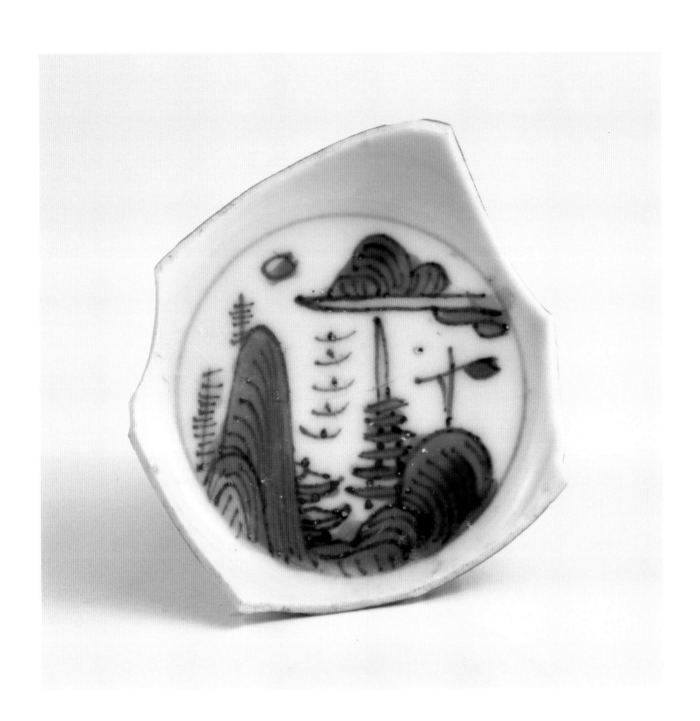